Restoring Your Life After Infidelity

A Guide for Adults to Heal, Rebuild, and Thrive Beyond Betrayal

Vivian Sterling

Table of Content

Introduction

In my 40s, I faced a series of events that left me shattered on every level—emotionally, physically, financially, and spiritually. The love of my life, my home, and even my health were ripped away from me in an instant. The person I trusted most, the one I envisioned spending my future with, betrayed me in a way I never imagined possible.

I was completely unaware of the double life my fiancé was leading. While I was working long hours on a tech project that consumed my days, another woman was living in my home, sharing my bed, and eating my food. It was like a twisted version of the Goldilocks story, except this wasn't a fairytale—it was my life unraveling before my eyes.

Every day, I left for work with a sense of purpose, eager to contribute to something meaningful and looking forward to our future together. My world seemed bright and full of promise. But beneath the surface, there was a storm brewing that I couldn't see.

The first crack appeared when my fiancé, who had always been loving and supportive, suddenly became aggressive. I was blindsided by his outburst, but the true blow came when I visited the doctor and was diagnosed with a severe sexually transmitted disease. The shock and confusion were overwhelming because I had only been intimate with him. How could this have happened?

As the truth slowly came to light, I discovered that my fiancé's aggression was no accident. It was part of a calculated plan. The other woman in his life wanted everything that was mine—my fiancé, my home, my life. She was willing to do whatever it took to get it. My fiancé, blinded by the allure of something new and exciting, went along with her scheme, betraying everything we had built together.

The weight of this betrayal crushed me. I felt my strength drain away, leaving me powerless to fight for my rights. To make matters worse, I was already battling cervical cancer, and the emotional toll of these events was more than I could bear. I couldn't muster the energy to stand up for myself and reclaim what was rightfully mine.

In the end, they faced no consequences for their actions. They stayed in the home I had worked so hard to buy until it was sold, while I was forced to move back in with my parents, making a long and exhausting commute to work every day. The injustice of it all was suffocating, but I was too broken to resist.

This experience left me with scars that I would carry for years. But it also set me on a path to understanding the deep psychological impact of betrayal and infidelity—what I would come to recognize as Post-Infidelity Stress Disorder (PISD). During my healing journey, I realized that I wasn't alone, and that there were others who had suffered similar trauma. This book is a result of that journey, a guide for those who are navigating the same treacherous waters, and a testament to the resilience of the human spirit.

Chapter 1

Understanding Post-Infidelity Stress Disorder (PISD)

Infidelity is more than a breach of trust—it can destroy your self-image, reality, and mental health. When someone you love and trust betrays you in such a profound way, the impact can be overwhelming, leading to what many experts now recognize as post-infidelity stress disorder (PISD). This chapter explores the nature of PISD, its root causes, and how it mirrors other forms of trauma.

A Journey through the Storm: My Story

I had always seen my marriage as a safe haven, a sanctuary from the chaos of the world. My relationship with Tom was built on years of shared dreams and mutual trust. So, when I stumbled upon evidence of his infidelity, my world as I knew it crumbled.

The initial shock left me numb. It was as if my entire reality had been torn apart in an instant. Every moment of our life together, every memory, seemed tainted by the betrayal. The emotional pain was overwhelming, and I found myself spiraling into a state of disbelief and profound sadness.

It felt as though the person I had trusted most had shattered my very sense of self.

My reaction was intense, mirroring the symptoms of Post-Infidelity Stress Disorder (PISD) described in this chapter. I replayed the discovery over and over in my mind, obsessively questioning every detail of Tom's affair. The intrusive thoughts consumed my days and nights, leaving me exhausted and unable to focus on anything else.

I found myself hyper-vigilant, constantly on edge, and suspicious of every interaction Tom had. The trust I once had was replaced with a gnawing fear of betrayal at every turn. I checked his phone, scrutinized his whereabouts, and doubted even the smallest gestures of kindness. This heightened state of alert was draining and strained our already fragile relationship even further.

Avoidance became my coping mechanism. I avoided places where I suspected Tom might have been with his affair partner, and I distanced myself from mutual friends who might have known about the betrayal. I even withdrew emotionally, shutting down conversations about the affair and the hurt I felt.

While this avoidance provided temporary relief, it also prevented me from processing my emotions and moving towards healing.

In my darkest moments, I felt emotionally numb. The joy and love I once experienced seemed distant and unreachable. This emotional numbing was my mind's way of shielding me from the overwhelming pain, but it also led to a profound sense of isolation and disconnection from those around me.

My journey through PISD was also marked by vivid flashbacks and nightmares. I frequently relived the moment of discovery and dreamt about Tom's betrayal in excruciating detail. These experiences were not just distressing—they were a constant reminder of the trauma I had endured.

Recognizing that my reactions were similar to those experienced in PTSD was both validating and daunting. It helped me understand that my suffering was not just a personal failing but a serious condition deserving of attention and care. This realization was the first step towards seeking support and healing.

My vulnerability to PISD was influenced by several factors. My anxious attachment style made me particularly susceptible to internalizing the betrayal and amplifying my feelings of worthlessness. My history of past traumas, including childhood experiences of abandonment, further intensified my emotional response. The intense nature of my relationship with Tom, coupled with a fragile sense of self-esteem, made the betrayal feel even more devastating.

However, my journey towards healing began when I acknowledged these factors and sought help. I reached out to a therapist who specialized in trauma and began attending support groups for individuals dealing with infidelity. Through therapy, I learned to challenge my negative self-beliefs and to reframe my perception of the betrayal. I also began practicing self-care and engaged in activities that helped rebuild my sense of self-worth.

Building a strong support network was crucial in my recovery. I leaned on close friends and family members who provided emotional support and helped me navigate the difficult path towards healing. I also found solace in writing and journaling, which allowed me to process my feelings and gain clarity.

Over time, my healing journey involved reconciling with my own emotions, rebuilding trust in myself, and gradually finding a new sense of security. I learned that while the road to recovery was long and challenging, it was also a path to self-discovery and empowerment.

My story is a testament to the resilience of the human spirit and the power of seeking support in the face of profound betrayal. My experience underscores the importance of understanding PISD and addressing the emotional and psychological impacts of infidelity with compassion and care.

The Root Causes of Intense Reactions to Infidelity

When infidelity occurs, it strikes at the very core of your emotional security. The person you trusted most has violated that trust, leaving you feeling exposed, vulnerable, and unsafe. This betrayal triggers a cascade of intense emotional reactions, often including shock, disbelief, anger, sadness, and a profound sense of loss.

These emotions can be so powerful that they overwhelm your ability to cope, leading to symptoms similar to those experienced by individuals with PTSD.

One of the primary reasons infidelity causes such intense reactions is because it disrupts your sense of reality. You may have believed that your relationship was solid, that your partner was faithful, and that your future together was secure. When you discover that your partner has been unfaithful, that reality is shattered. Suddenly, everything you thought you knew is called into question, leaving you feeling lost and disoriented.

The emotional pain of infidelity is compounded by the feelings of rejection and worthlessness that often accompany it. You may begin to doubt your own worth, wondering what you did wrong or why you weren't enough for your partner. These feelings can be incredibly damaging to your self-esteem and lead to a deep sense of shame and shame.

Additionally, infidelity often leads to a sense of betrayal trauma, a specific type of trauma that occurs when someone you depend on for survival and emotional support violates your trust. This type of trauma is particularly intense because it affects your ability to feel safe and secure in relationships, not just with your partner, but with others as well.

Similarities between PISD and Post-Traumatic Stress Disorder (PTSD)

Post-Infidelity Stress Disorder (PISD) and Post-Traumatic Stress Disorder (PTSD) share many similarities, as both involve a response to a deeply distressing or disturbing experience. While PTSD is typically associated with life-threatening events such as war, natural disasters, or violent assaults, PISD arises from the emotional and psychological trauma caused by betrayal in a close relationship. Despite the differences in their origins, the symptoms of PISD often mirror those of PTSD, making it a serious and debilitating condition.

One of the most prominent similarities between PISD and PTSD is the presence of intrusive thoughts. After discovering infidelity, you might find yourself obsessively replaying the moment you came out, questioning the details of the affair, or imagining the events that took place behind your back. These intrusive thoughts can be relentless, making it difficult to focus on anything else and preventing you from finding peace.

Another common symptom is hypervigilance, which is a state of being constantly on edge or alert. In the context of PISD, this might manifest as a heightened suspicion of your partner or a fear of being deceived again. You may find yourself frequently checking their phone, questioning their whereabouts, or doubting their honesty in even the smallest matters. This hypervigilance can be exhausting and can further strain an already damaged relationship.

Avoidance is also a key symptom in both PISD and PTSD. In an attempt to protect yourself from further pain, you may avoid situations, conversations, or even people that remind you of the betrayal.

This could mean avoiding places where you suspect the affair took situation, steering clear of mutual friends who may have known about the infidelity, or shutting down emotionally to avoid dealing with the hurt. While avoidance might provide temporary relief, it often prolongs the healing process by preventing you from confronting and processing your emotions.

Emotional numbness is another shared characteristic. After such a traumatic betrayal, you might feel disconnected from your emotions or unable to experience joy, love, or even anger in the way you did before. This emotional numbing is a protective mechanism, your mind's way of shielding you from overwhelming pain. Struggle to connect with others and your own feelings can lead to isolation.

In both cases, flashbacks and nightmares are also common. You might recall the moment of discovery or dream about the betrayal in vivid detail, which can be distressing and lead to sleep disturbances.

These experiences are not just memories but are often accompanied by the same intense emotions you felt at the time of the original trauma.

Both PISD and PTSD can lead to a deep sense of mistrust, not just in the person who betrayed you but in people in general. This mistrust can make it difficult to form new relationships or to fully invest in existing ones, as you may constantly fear being hurt again.

Understanding the similarities between PISD and PTSD is crucial because it validates the intense emotional and psychological pain that infidelity can cause. It also underscores the need for appropriate treatment and support, as PISD is not just a "relationship issue," but a serious condition that can have long-lasting effects on your mental health and well-being.

Factors Contributing to Vulnerability to PISD

Not everyone who experiences infidelity will develop Post-Infidelity Stress Disorder (PISD). Various factors contribute to an individual's vulnerability to PISD, shaping how they respond to the trauma of betrayal. Understanding these factors can help you understand your reactions and why infidelity affects you so much.

1. Attachment Style: Your attachment style, which is formed in early childhood based on your relationships with your primary caregivers, plays a significant role in how you respond to infidelity.

People with a secure attachment style typically have a strong sense of self-worth and trust in others. While they may still experience intense pain following betrayal, they are often better equipped to process their emotions and seek support. If you have an anxious or avoidant attachment style, PISD may be more likely. Anxiously attached individuals often fear abandonment and may be more likely to internalize the betrayal, blaming themselves and experiencing heightened anxiety.

Avoidant attached individuals, on the other hand, may struggle with trust issues and find it difficult to reconnect emotionally after infidelity, leading to prolonged distress.

2. **Previous trauma or abuse**. A history of trauma or abuse can significantly increase your susceptibility to PISD. If you've experienced past betrayals, whether in romantic relationships, friendships, or even within your family, the pain of infidelity can reopen old wounds and intensify your emotional response. If you have experienced any type of abuse, the betrayal of infidelity can intensify feelings of powerlessness and fear, making it even more challenging to cope.

3. **Self-esteem and self-worth**: Your sense of self-esteem and self-worth also plays a crucial role in how you react to infidelity. If your self-esteem is already fragile, the betrayal can feel like confirmation of your deepest fears—that you are unworthy of love, respect, or loyalty.

   This can lead to a downward spiral of self-blame and self-loathing, making it difficult to recover from the emotional trauma. On the other hand, if you have a strong sense of self-worth, you might still be devastated by infidelity, but you are more likely to view it as a reflection of your partner's flaws rather than your own. This perspective can help you maintain your sense of identity and resilience in the face of betrayal.

4. **The Nature of the Relationship:** Your relationship's dynamics prior to the betrayal can influence your vulnerability to PISD. If your relationship was particularly close or intense, the betrayal might feel like an even greater violation, leading to a more severe emotional response. Similarly, if you had invested a tremendous deal of time, energy, and hope into the relationship, the loss of that future can feel overwhelming, making it harder to move forward.

In contrast, if the relationship was already strained or distant, the betrayal might be less surprising but still painful. However, the shock and trauma might be mitigated by a sense of inevitability, reducing the likelihood of developing PISD.

5. **Social Support**: The level of support you have from friends, family, and your community can significantly affect how you cope with infidelity. Strong social support can provide you with the emotional resources you need to process the betrayal and begin healing. Conversely, if you feel isolated or lack a support system, the impact of the betrayal can be magnified, increasing your vulnerability to PISD.

6. **Coping Mechanisms:** Your natural coping mechanisms, whether adaptive or maladaptive, also play a role in how you respond to infidelity. Adaptive coping mechanisms, such as seeking therapy, talking to trusted friends, or engaging in self-care, can help you process the trauma in a healthy way. However, if you rely on maladaptive coping mechanisms, such as denial, substance abuse, or self-isolation, you may find yourself stuck in a cycle of pain and unable to move forward.

7. **Cultural and societal influences:** Cultural and societal expectations about relationships, gender roles, and fidelity can influence your response to infidelity. In some cultures, there may be a strong stigma attached to being cheated on, leading to feelings of shame and humiliation that exacerbate the emotional impact. In other cases, societal pressures to forgive and move on might make you feel guilty for your pain, compounding your distress.

Understanding these factors can help you recognize why you may be struggling to cope with infidelity and why the emotional toll might be particularly severe. It's important to remember that PISD is not a sign of weakness but a natural response to a deeply traumatic event. Recognizing these contributing factors allows you to begin taking steps toward healing and recovery.

Chapter 2

Seeking Professional Help for PISD

Navigating the aftermath of infidelity is an overwhelming experience, and the emotional toll it takes can be immense. For many, the pain and distress may be too much to handle alone. Seeking professional help is often a crucial step in the healing process, especially when symptoms of Post-Infidelity Stress Disorder (PISD) are present. In this chapter, we'll explore when to consider therapy, the different therapeutic approaches available, and how they can aid in your recovery.

Personal Journey to Healing: Overcoming Infidelity with Professional Help

When I found out about the infidelity, my world shattered into pieces. The pain was unbearable, and I felt as though I was trapped in an endless spiral of despair and confusion. I knew I couldn't navigate this alone, so I decided to seek professional help. The journey to healing wasn't easy, but it was transformative, and it started with acknowledging that I needed support.

In the early days after discovering the betrayal, I was plagued by persistent intrusive thoughts. My mind replayed the betrayal on a loop, making it impossible to focus on anything else. I experienced hypervigilance, constantly second-guessing everyone around me. Trust, once a given, became a distant memory. I knew it was time to seek help when these symptoms began interfering with my daily life and well-being.

My first step was Cognitive-Behavioral Therapy (CBT). I met with a therapist who specialized in trauma and PISD. Through CBT, I learned to challenge the negative thoughts that had taken root in my mind. I used to believe that the betrayal was a reflection of my worth, that I was to blame, and that trust was a lost cause. CBT helped me reframe these distorted beliefs.

With my therapist's guidance, I began to recognize and challenge these thoughts, learning to view the situation with a more balanced perspective. In addition to CBT, I explored Eye Movement Desensitization and Reprocessing (EMDR). During these sessions, I focused on the traumatic memories while following guided eye movements. The process was both surreal and liberating. EMDR helped me reduce the emotional intensity of those memories.

I began to experience fewer flashbacks and nightmares, which allowed me to regain control over my emotional responses. Reprocessing the trauma helped me rebuild a sense of self and envision a future beyond the betrayal.

My therapy journey also included trauma-informed care. This approach created a safe and validating environment where I felt understood and supported. My therapist was attuned to the pervasive impact of the trauma and ensured that our sessions did not inadvertently re-traumatize me. This approach helped me feel empowered and provided a holistic view of my experiences, enabling me to see the broader context of my life and how the betrayal had affected me.

Alongside individual therapy, I joined a support group for individuals dealing with infidelity. The shared experiences and empathy from the group members were incredibly validating. Hearing others share their stories and insights provided me with comfort and practical advice. The sense of community and connection was a crucial part of my healing process, reminding me that I was not alone in this journey.

At certain points, I struggled with severe anxiety and insomnia, which made it difficult to engage fully in therapy. My healthcare provider recommended medication to help stabilize my mood and alleviate some of the more intense symptoms. This allowed me to focus better during therapy sessions and engage more effectively with the healing process. Medication became a supplementary tool that, combined with therapy, supported my overall recovery.

Looking back, seeking professional help was one of the most courageous and beneficial decisions I made. Each therapeutic approach offered unique support and contributed to my healing in different ways. From reframing my thoughts with CBT to reprocessing trauma with EMDR, and finding solace in support groups, every step of the journey brought me closer to recovery. The combination of therapy, support, and medication allowed me to move forward, rebuild trust, and reclaim my sense of self.

If you find yourself in a similar place, remember that professional help can offer the guidance and support needed to navigate the aftermath of infidelity and find your path to healing.

When to Consider Therapy

Deciding whether or not to seek therapy after experiencing infidelity is a deeply personal choice, but certain signs indicate that professional help may be necessary. If you find yourself struggling to function in your daily life, therapy can provide you with the support and tools needed to cope with your emotions and begin healing. Some signs that it might be time to seek therapy include:

- Persistent Intrusive Thoughts: If you're constantly replaying the betrayal in your mind or experiencing flashbacks that disrupt your day-to-day activities, therapy can help you manage these intrusive thoughts.
- Hypervigilance and Trust Issues: If you're unable to trust your partner or anyone else, constantly feeling on edge or suspicious, a therapist can work with you to rebuild trust and security.
- Emotional Numbness: If you feel disconnected from your emotions or are unable to experience joy, love, or even anger, therapy can help you reconnect with your feelings in a safe and controlled environment.

- Avoidance Behaviors: If you're avoiding situations, people, or conversations that remind you of your infidelity, therapy can help you confront and process your emotions rather than suppress them.

- Depression and Anxiety: If you're experiencing symptoms of depression, anxiety, or panic attacks, professional support can be essential in managing these conditions and preventing them from worsening.

- Difficulty Making Decisions: If you struggle to decide whether to stay or leave your relationship, therapy can provide clarity and guidance in navigating these difficult choices.

- Impact on Physical Health: If your physical health is suffering—whether through loss of appetite, insomnia, or chronic stress—therapy can help address the underlying emotional causes and promote overall well-being.

Therapy can help anyone who feels stuck or overwhelmed with no idea how to proceed. Whether you're dealing with intense emotional pain, confusion, or a sense of numbness, a therapist can offer a safe space to explore your feelings and develop a plan for healing.

Therapeutic Approaches for Healing PISD

When dealing with Post-Infidelity Stress Disorder (PISD), choosing the right therapeutic approach can make a significant difference in your recovery journey. There are several evidence-based therapies designed to help you process the trauma, rebuild your sense of self, and regain control over your life. This section explores various therapeutic approaches, each offering unique benefits tailored to different aspects of PISD.

Cognitive-Behavioral Therapy (CBT)

Cognitive-behavioral therapy (CBT) is one of the most widely used approaches for treating trauma-related conditions like PISD. CBT focuses on identifying and challenging the negative thoughts and beliefs that arise after infidelity, which often contribute to feelings of worthlessness, guilt, or anxiety.

In CBT, you work with a therapist to recognize the cognitive distortions that may be amplifying your distress. For example, you might believe that the betrayal was your fault or that you'll never be able to trust anyone again. Through CBT, you learn to reframe these thoughts in a more realistic and compassionate way. By changing your thought patterns, you can begin to alter your emotional responses and behaviors, making it easier to cope with the pain of betrayal.

CBT also involves practical strategies for managing symptoms like intrusive thoughts, hypervigilance, and avoidance. Your therapist might teach you techniques such as grounding exercises, mindfulness, and relaxation methods to help you stay present and reduce anxiety. Over time, these tools can help you regain a sense of control and stability in your life.

2. **Eye Movement Desensitization and Reprocessing (EMDR):** Eye Movement Desensitization and Reprocessing (EMDR) is another effective therapy for treating trauma, including PISD. The foundation of EMDR is the theory that painful memories may become "stuck" in the brain and cause persistent pain.

This therapy uses a combination of guided eye movements and cognitive processing to help reprocess these memories, reducing their emotional intensity and allowing you to integrate them in a healthier way.

During an EMDR session, your therapist will ask you to focus on specific aspects of the traumatic memory while following a series of eye movements. This process helps to unlock and reprocess the memory, making it less distressing.

EMDR has been shown to be particularly effective for individuals who experience flashbacks, nightmares, or other intrusive symptoms related to PISD.

EMDR can also help you build new, positive associations and beliefs about yourself and your future, which can be empowering after experiencing such a profound betrayal. By reprocessing the trauma, you can begin to heal and move forward with a greater sense of peace and resilience.

3.   **Trauma-Informed Care**

Trauma-Informed Care is an approach that recognizes the pervasive impact of trauma on an individual's life and emphasizes creating a therapeutic environment that is safe, supportive, and empowering. This approach is not a specific therapy but rather a framework that guides how therapy is delivered.

In a trauma-informed setting, your therapist will be particularly sensitive to the effects of infidelity trauma, ensuring that the therapeutic process does not re-traumatize you. This approach involves validating your experiences, fostering a sense of safety, and empowering you to control your healing journey.

Trauma-Informed Care also emphasizes the importance of understanding the broader context of your life, including your past experiences, relationships, and coping mechanisms. This holistic perspective can help you make sense of your reactions to infidelity and provide you with the tools to rebuild your life in a way that feels safe and authentic.

4.   Support Groups

Support groups offer a communal approach to healing, providing a space where you can connect with others who have experienced similar betrayals. In a support group, you can share your story, hear from others who are going through similar challenges, and gain insight from their experiences.

The shared understanding and empathy found in support groups can be incredibly validating, reducing feelings of isolation and shame. Support groups can also provide practical advice and coping strategies, as well as emotional support during difficult times. For many, the sense of community and connection that comes from participating in a support group is an essential part of the healing process.

5.   Medication

In some cases, medication may be recommended as part of your treatment plan for PISD, particularly if you are experiencing severe symptoms of anxiety, depression, or insomnia. Antidepressants, anti-anxiety medications, or sleep aids can help alleviate some of the more intense symptoms, allowing you to engage more fully in therapy and other healing activities.

Medication is typically most effective when used in conjunction with therapy, as it can help stabilize your mood and reduce distress, making it easier to process your emotions and work through the trauma. However, it's important to discuss the potential benefits and risks of medication with a healthcare provider, as well as any concerns you may have.

Chapter 3

Self-care Techniques for Managing PISD

ealing from Post-Infidelity Stress Disorder (PISD) is a journey that requires not only professional support but also a commitment to self-care. Taking care of yourself during this difficult time is essential for rebuilding your emotional and physical well-being. In this chapter, we'll explore various self-care techniques that can help you manage the symptoms of PISD, nurture your inner strength, and gradually restore your sense of peace and balance.

Personal Story: Finding Strength through Self-Care

After discovering the betrayal of infidelity, I felt as though my world had come crashing down. The pain was overwhelming, and it seemed impossible to imagine a future free from the shadows of heartbreak and self-doubt. Yet, amidst the chaos, I knew that to heal and reclaim my life, I had to prioritize my well-being. Here's how self-care became my lifeline during this tumultuous period.

In the early days of the aftermath, my body felt like a stranger. My eating habits had grown irregular, and I was completely weary. Recognizing that physical health was the foundation of my recovery, I decided to take small but deliberate steps towards self-care.

I started with regular exercise, initially as a way to combat the lethargy that accompanied my emotional distress. I began with simple daily walks, gradually incorporating yoga and more intense workouts. Each session left me feeling more grounded and capable. Exercise became my sanctuary—a place where I could process my emotions and regain my strength.

Nutrition played a crucial role as well. I began focusing on balanced meals, incorporating fruits, vegetables, and lean proteins. I noticed that avoiding excessive caffeine and sugar helped stabilize my mood and provided a more consistent energy level throughout the day. The improvement in my physical well-being was a beacon of hope amidst the pain.

Sleep was another area I had to address. I established a consistent sleep routine, creating a calming ritual each night. Reading before bed and using soft, soothing music helped signal to my body that it was time to rest.

This small change made a significant difference in my overall emotional stability.

Allowing myself to grieve was an essential part of my healing process. I began journaling my thoughts and emotions, which provided a safe outlet for my grief. Talking to a trusted friend also helped me navigate the complex emotions I was experiencing. Grieving was challenging, but it was also necessary for my healing.

Setting boundaries was another crucial step. I had to limit contact with my partner to avoid painful conversations that I wasn't ready for. This decision was difficult but essential for my emotional health. It allowed me to create space for healing without the constant reminders of my betrayal.

Creative expression became a lifeline. I turned to painting and writing as ways to process my feelings. Art provided a means to explore and articulate emotions that were otherwise difficult to express. This creative outlet helped me find meaning and healing in the midst of my pain.

Practicing self-compassion was perhaps the most transformative aspect of my emotional self-care. I learned to speak to myself with kindness, recognizing that healing was a journey that required patience. I reminded myself that I was worthy of love and compassion, despite the pain I was experiencing.

Infidelity left me feeling as though I had lost a part of myself. To rebuild my sense of identity, I revisited hobbies that had once brought me joy. I started painting again and took up hiking, activities that helped me reconnect with the parts of myself that had been overshadowed by the betrayal.

Setting personal goals was another way to regain a sense of purpose. I decided to pursue further education and set small milestones for myself. Each accomplishment, no matter how minor, contributed to a growing sense of confidence and direction.

Surrounding myself with supportive people was invaluable. I reached out to friends and family who uplifted and encouraged me. Their support reminded me of my worth and helped me feel less isolated in my journey.

Exploring my values helped me regain clarity about what mattered most to me. Reflecting on my core beliefs and priorities provided a strong foundation as I navigated the challenges of rebuilding my life.

My living space became a crucial part of my healing journey. I decluttered and simplified my home, removing items that reminded me of the pain and creating a more serene environment. Adding calming elements, like soft lighting and soothing scents, made my space more comforting.

I designated a specific area in my home as a personal sanctuary. It became a retreat where I could relax and recharge. This space was essential for my emotional recovery, providing a haven where I could find peace and solace.

Mindfulness became a daily practice. I started with mindful breathing exercises, which helped me stay grounded in the present moment. This practice was a powerful tool for managing overwhelming emotions and reducing stress.

Mindful movement, like yoga and tai chi, also became part of my routine. These activities helped me connect with my body and foster a sense of balance. Mindful observation of my surroundings allowed me to appreciate the beauty in everyday moments, helping me shift my focus from the pain to the present.

Despite the challenges, I made a conscious effort to cultivate positivity. Gratitude journaling became a daily ritual. I wrote down small things I was grateful for, which helped me focus on the positive aspects of my life.

Affirmations played a role in reinforcing my self-worth and potential. Repeating statements like "I am strong" and "I deserve happiness" helped shift my mindset towards a more positive outlook.

Seeking out moments of joy became a priority. I made an effort to engage in activities that brought me happiness, whether it was listening to a favorite song or spending time with loved ones. These moments of joy provided much-needed relief from the pain and reminded me of life's beauty.

Through these self-care techniques, I was able to navigate the journey of healing from infidelity. Each practice, from prioritizing physical health to embracing positivity, contributed to my recovery and helped me rebuild a sense of peace and balance in my life

1.   Prioritizing Your Physical Health

When dealing with the aftermath of infidelity, your physical health can often take a backseat to emotional turmoil. However, taking care of your body is crucial for managing stress and maintaining overall well-being. Crucial aspects to consider include:

Exercise Regularly: Physical activity is a powerful tool for reducing stress, improving mood, and increasing energy levels. Whether it's a daily walk, yoga, or a more intense workout, regular exercise can help you release pent-up emotions and clear your mind.

Healthy Eating: Nourishing your body with balanced meals can help stabilize your mood and provide the energy you need to cope with stress. Try to incorporate a variety of fruits, vegetables, whole grains, and lean proteins into your diet, and avoid excessive consumption of caffeine, sugar, and alcohol, which can exacerbate anxiety and depression.

Sleep Hygiene: Quality sleep is essential for emotional regulation and overall health. Establish a regular sleep routine by setting a consistent bedtime and wake-up time each day. Create a calming bedtime ritual, such as reading or listening to soothing music, to signal to your body that it's time to wind down.

Mind-Body Practices: Techniques like deep breathing, progressive muscle relaxation, or mindfulness meditation can help calm your nervous system and reduce the physical symptoms of stress. These practices can also increase your awareness of the present moment, making it easier to manage overwhelming emotions.

2.   Emotional Self-Care

Caring for your emotional well-being is a critical aspect of managing PISD. This involves acknowledging your feelings, expressing them in healthy ways, and cultivating a sense of inner peace.

Allow Yourself to Grieve: Infidelity represents a profound loss—the loss of trust, security, and the future you envisioned. It's important to give yourself permission to grieve this loss, whether through journaling, talking to a friend, or simply allowing yourself to feel the sadness. It's normal for grieving to occur throughout the healing process.

Set Boundaries: After infidelity, you may need to establish new boundaries to protect your emotional health. This could mean limiting contact with your partner, especially if you're not ready to have certain conversations, or distancing yourself from people or situations that trigger painful memories.

Engage in Creative Expression: Channeling your emotions into creative activities, such as writing, painting, or playing music, can be a powerful way to process your feelings. Creative expression allows you to explore your inner world, release emotions that might be difficult to articulate, and find meaning in your experiences.

Self-compassion means treating yourself with the same kindness and understanding that you would extend to a close friend. Remind yourself that you are human, that healing takes time, and that you deserve patience and care.

3.   Rebuilding your sense of identity

Infidelity can leave you feeling lost and unsure of who you are. Reconnecting with yourself and rebuilding your sense of identity is an important part of the healing process.

Reconnect with Your Passions: revisit hobbies, interests, or activities that brought you joy before the bet. Activities you enjoy can help you regain your self-confidence and recognize your strengths..

Set Personal Goals: Setting and working towards personal goals can help you regain a sense of purpose and direction. Whether it's pursuing a new skill, advancing your career, or improving your health, achieving small milestones can boost your confidence and provide a sense of accomplishment.

Surround Yourself with Supportive People: Seek out friends, family, or communities that uplift and support you. Being surrounded by positive and understanding people can help you feel valued and remind you of your worth outside of the relationship.

Explore Your Values: Reflect on what's essential to you— your values, beliefs, and what you stand for. Exploring and affirming your core values can provide a strong foundation as you rebuild your life.

4.   Creating a Healing Environment

The environment you create for yourself can have a profound impact on your healing process. Making your living space a place of comfort and tranquility can help you feel more secure and at peace.

Declutter and simplify: A cluttered space can contribute to feelings of overwhelm and stress. Take some time to declutter your home, removing items that no longer serve you and creating a more organized, serene environment.

Incorporate Calming Elements: Add elements to your space that promote relaxation and well-being, such as soft lighting, comfortable seating, or soothing scents.

You might also consider incorporating elements of nature, like plants or natural materials, to bring a sense of calm and grounding. Establish a Sanctuary: Designate a specific area in your home as a personal sanctuary where you can retreat when you need to relax and recharge. This could be a cozy corner with a favorite chair and a relaxing book, or a space for meditation and reflection.

Cultivating mindfulness and present-moment awareness: Mindfulness is the practice of staying present and fully engaged in the current moment, without judgment. It can be a powerful tool for managing the overwhelming emotions that come with PISD.

Mindful Breathing: Mindful breathing is one of the easiest ways to practice mindfulness. Take a few minutes each day to focus on your breath, noticing the sensation of air moving in and out of your body. By using this technique, you may learn to relax and focus on the here and now.

Mindful Movement: You may improve your connection to your body and the present moment by engaging in practices like yoga, tai chi, or simply mindful walking.

These practices encourage you to move with intention and awareness, fostering a sense of peace and balance.

Mindful observation: Spend a few moments each day observing your surroundings with full attention. Whether it's the beauty of nature, the details of a room, or the sounds around you, mindful observation helps you appreciate the present and reduce rumination.

Embracing positivity and gratitude: While it may be challenging to find positivity in the midst of pain, cultivating a mindset of gratitude and focusing on positive aspects of life can significantly aid in healing.

Gratitude Journaling: List a few things for which you are thankful every day in your journal. Simple things like a warm cup of tea, encouraging words from friends, or a quiet time might serve as these. Focusing on gratitude helps shift your attention away from the pain and towards the good that still exists in your life.

Affirmations: Positive affirmations are statements that confirm your strengths, worth, and potential. Repeating affirmations like "I am strong," "I deserve happiness," or "I am healing every day" can reinforce a positive mindset and build your self-esteem.

Seek Out Joy: Actively look for moments of joy, no matter how small. It could be listening to a favorite song, spending time outdoors, or connecting with a loved one. These moments of joy can help counterbalance the pain and remind you that life still holds beauty and happiness.

Chapter 4

Deciding on Your Relationship Future

One of the hardest decisions after infidelity is whether to stay or leave. This decision is deeply personal and can be fraught with emotional turmoil, confusion, and fear of the unknown. In this chapter, we'll explore the factors you might consider when deciding on your relationship future, provide guidance on breaking up with a cheater if that's the path you choose, and discuss strategies for moving forward with clarity and confidence.

Finding My Path: A Personal Journey through the Infidelity Decision

After discovering my partner's infidelity, I found myself lost in a whirlwind of emotions. The initial shock gave way to a deep, aching hurt that seemed impossible to move past. The questions swirling in my mind were relentless: Should I stay or leave? Could this relationship be salvaged, or was it time to move on?

I knew that before making any decision, I needed to take a step back and reflect on my feelings and needs. I asked myself a series of questions that felt both daunting and necessary.

What do I feel in my heart? I was overwhelmed with a profound sense of betrayal. But as I sat quietly, trying to tune into my heart, I noticed a small, flickering hope that maybe, just maybe, forgiveness was possible.

What would make me feel safe and secure? I realized that honesty and transparency were crucial for me to even consider staying. I needed a commitment from my partner that this would not happen again, and a genuine effort to rebuild trust.

What are my values? Fidelity was a core value for me, and the betrayal felt like a direct assault on my principles. I questioned whether I could ever truly rebuild trust with someone who had broken it so fundamentally.

What does my intuition tell me? My intuition was a mix of fear and hope. It whispered that if my partner was genuinely remorseful and committed to change, there might be a path forward. But it also warned me not to ignore the profound hurt I was feeling.

After reflecting on my own needs, I began to evaluate the relationship more objectively. Is my partner genuinely remorseful? My partner's apology was filled with regret, and they were committed to making amends. They began attending counseling and showed a willingness to change, which gave me a glimmer of hope.

Is there a history of dishonesty or betrayal? Fortunately, this was not a recurring pattern. However, the betrayal had shaken me deeply, and I needed to be certain that it was an isolated incident and not a sign of deeper, unresolved issues.

Are we both willing to work on the relationship? We both committed to open communication and counseling. This mutual effort to heal the relationship was encouraging and made me consider the possibility of moving forward together.

Can I envision a future together? Imagining a future with my partner was challenging. The pain of betrayal was still raw, but I could see potential for rebuilding our lives together if we worked diligently on our relationship.

Breaking Up with a Cheater: My Decision

Despite the efforts and possibilities, I came to the realization that the relationship could not be salvaged. Breaking up was heart-wrenching, but it was clear that moving on was the healthier choice for both of us.

Planning for Safety and Support I ensured I had a safe place to go and reached out to friends and family for support. I needed to protect myself emotionally and physically during this challenging time.

Being Clear and Direct When I ended the relationship, I was firm and direct. I expressed my decision calmly, ensuring there was no ambiguity. This clarity helped both of us start the process of moving on. Setting Boundaries Post-breakup, I established boundaries to protect my emotional well-being. I limited contact with my ex-partner and focused on healing without the added stress of continued interaction.

Allowing Myself to Grieve I allowed myself to grieve the loss of the relationship. I felt a mix of sadness and relief, and I gave myself the space to process these emotions without rushing the healing process.

Prioritizing My Healing I continued practicing the self-care techniques I had learned. I sought additional support through counseling and support groups, which helped me navigate this new chapter with greater resilience.

- Moving Forward with Clarity and Confidence
- The journey through infidelity was challenging, but it led me to a place of greater self-awareness and strength.
- Trusting Myself I learned to trust my intuition and my decision-making process. It was difficult, but I knew I was making the best choice for my well-being.
- Staying Open to New Possibilities Moving forward, I kept my heart open to new possibilities. I embraced personal growth and the opportunity to build a future filled with joy and new relationships.
- Surrounding Myself with Positivity I surrounded myself with supportive and positive people. Their encouragement helped me rebuild my confidence and sense of self-worth as I began this new chapter of my life.

- This journey was not easy, but it was a path to healing and personal growth. I learned that, while the pain of betrayal would always be a part of my past, it did not define my future. Through self-reflection, setting boundaries, and trusting myself, I found the clarity and confidence to move forward with hope and resilience.

- Reflecting on Your Feelings and Needs

- Before making any decisions, it's essential to take time to reflect on your own feelings and needs. Infidelity can leave you feeling hurt, betrayed, and unsure of what you want or need from a relationship moving forward. As you think about it, consider these questions:

- What do you feel in your heart? Pay attention to your emotions. Do you feel a deep sense of hurt that you can't move past, or is there a part of you that believes in the possibility of forgiveness and reconciliation?

- What does it take to feel safe and secure? Consider what it would take for you to feel safe in the relationship again. Do you need honesty, transparency, or a commitment to change? Or do you feel that the betrayal has irrevocably shattered your sense of safety?

- What are your values? Reflect on your core values and how they align with the relationship. Is fidelity a non-negotiable value for you?

Can you see yourself rebuilding trust with your partner, or do you feel that the infidelity has crossed an unforgivable line?

- What does your intuition tell you? Sometimes, your intuition can guide you more clearly than your thoughts. Is your inner voice telling you to stay and work things out or move on?
- Evaluating The Relationship's Potential for Healing
- After reflecting on your own feelings and needs, it's important to assess the relationship itself. This involves taking a realistic look at your partner's actions, the history of your relationship, and the potential for healing and rebuilding trust.
- Is your partner genuinely remorseful? A partner who truly regrets betrayal will apologize, show empathy, and do whatever it takes to make amends. If your partner is defensive, blames you, or minimizes the infidelity, it may be a sign that they're not fully committed to the healing process.
- Is there a history of dishonesty or betrayal? If this is not the first time your partner has betrayed your trust, it's important to consider whether a pattern of behavior is present. Repeated infidelity or dishonesty may indicate

deeper issues that are unlikely to be resolved without significant change.

- Can you both put forth some effort to improve your relationship? Healing from infidelity requires effort from both partners. If you're both committed to open communication, counseling, and rebuilding trust, there may be hope for reconciliation. If either of you is unwilling or unable to work, the relationship may be difficult to repair.

- Can you envision a future together? Imagine living with your partner in the years to come. Do you see a future where trust and happiness are restored, or do you feel that the pain of betrayal will always linger? Your ability to envision a positive future together can be a key indicator of whether the relationship is worth pursuing.

- Breaking Up with a Cheater: Considerations and Strategies

If you've decided that the relationship cannot be salvaged, breaking up with a cheater is often the next step. Ending a relationship, especially one that has been a significant part of your life, is never easy. Here's how to approach the process:

- Plan for Safety and Support: If your partner has shown signs of aggression or if you feel unsafe, it's crucial to plan your exit carefully. Ensure you have a safe place to go, whether it's staying with a friend or family member, and consider involving a support network to help you through the process.

- Be Clear and Direct: When breaking up, clarity is key. Express your decision calmly and directly, without leaving room for ambiguity. Let your partner know that the relationship is over and that your decision is final. Avoid prolonged discussions or arguments that may only cause more pain.

- Set Boundaries: After the breakup, it's important to establish boundaries to protect your emotional well-being. This might include limiting or cutting off contact with your ex-partner, particularly if they try to manipulate or guilt you into reconsidering your decision.

- Allow Yourself to Grieve: Even if breaking up is the right decision, it can still be incredibly painful. Allow yourself to grieve the loss of the relationship and the future you had envisioned together. It's normal to feel a range of emotions, from sadness to relief, and it's important to process these feelings at your own pace.

- Prioritize Your Healing: After the breakup, focus on your healing. Continue practicing the self-care techniques discussed in the previous chapter, and consider seeking additional support, such as counseling or support groups, to help you navigate this challenging time.

Moving Forward with Clarity and Confidence

- Whether you choose to stay in the relationship and work towards healing or decide to end things and move on, the most important thing is to make a decision that aligns with your values, needs, and long-term well-being.

- Trust Yourself: Trust that you are making the best decision for yourself, even if it's difficult. Your intuition, feelings, and reflections are valuable guides in navigating this complex situation.

- Stay Open to New Possibilities: Moving forward after infidelity can feel daunting, but it also opens up new possibilities for growth, self-discovery, and, eventually, new relationships. Keep your heart and mind open to the future, knowing that healing and happiness are within your reach.

- Surround Yourself with Positivity: As you move forward, surround yourself with people and experiences that bring positivity, support, and joy into your life. This will help you rebuild your confidence and sense of self-worth as you begin this new chapter.

Chapter 5

Rebuilding Trust after Infidelity

After my partner's betrayal, I found myself engulfed in a storm of emotions. The pain was palpable, and the future of our relationship seemed bleak. Yet, as we faced this crisis, we were both determined to navigate the path of healing. This chapter details our journey and the steps we took to rebuild trust and restore our relationship.

The first step we took was to confront the betrayal head-on. We sat down in a quiet room, away from distractions, and began the painful but necessary process of honest communication. I found it crucial to voice my hurt and confusion openly. I wanted answers to questions that had been gnawing at me since discovering the affair. My partner, on the other hand, had to be transparent and patient, answering each question and providing the clarity I needed.

I remember one particular night when I asked about the details of the affair, seeking to understand not out of anger but to find a way forward. My partner listened intently, acknowledging the impact of their actions.

This validation of my feelings was a turning point. It was clear that they truly understood the depth of my pain, and it helped me start to feel heard.

Taking responsibility was another critical step. My partner made a sincere effort to own up to their actions. It was not just about saying "I'm sorry" but demonstrating genuine remorse. They expressed regret for the hurt caused and took active steps to amend their behavior. This included attending therapy to understand the underlying issues that led to the infidelity and making significant changes in their approach to our relationship.

I appreciated their efforts to show empathy, not only by apologizing but by making amends through consistent actions. This included changing their routine to rebuild my trust and focusing on addressing the personal issues that contributed to the betrayal.

We decided that rebuilding trust required a new level of transparency. This meant open communication about everything from daily activities to emotional states. My partner agreed to share more about their whereabouts and any interactions that could be a source of insecurity for me.

Creating a trust-building plan was instrumental. We set clear expectations for communication and made a commitment to regular check-ins. These check-ins were crucial in helping us both stay informed about each other's feelings and progress. They also provided a structured way to address and resolve any lingering doubts or concerns.

Recognizing the complexity of our situation, we sought professional help. Couples counseling became a vital part of our healing process. In therapy, we were able to explore our feelings in a safe environment and learn effective strategies for rebuilding our relationship. Our therapist guided us through difficult conversations and helped us develop skills for better communication.

- Individual therapy also played a role. My partner worked on understanding their motivations and addressing personal issues, while I focused on processing my emotions and rebuilding my self-esteem. This dual approach allowed us both to work on our individual healing while supporting each other
- Rebuilding trust after infidelity is one of the hardest parts of healing. Trust, once broken, requires considerable effort and commitment from both partners to repair.

- It involves more than just addressing the immediate pain; it requires a deep, honest, and sustained effort to restore faith and security in the relationship. In this chapter, we'll explore the steps necessary to heal and restore trust, providing a roadmap for both partners to follow.

- **Acknowledging the Betrayal:** The first step in rebuilding trust is acknowledging the betrayal in its entirety. This involves recognizing the hurt and damage caused by the infidelity and understanding its impact on the relationship.

- **Honest Communication:** Both partners must engage in open and honest communication about what happened. The person who committed the betrayal should be willing to answer questions and provide clarity about the affair, while the betrayed partner should express their feelings and concerns openly.

- **Validation of Feelings**: For the partner who committed the betrayal, it is critical to validate their partner's feelings. This means acknowledging the pain, anger, and hurt without trying to minimize or deflect responsibility. Understanding the emotional impact of the betrayal is a key part of rebuilding trust.

- Taking Responsibility and Showing Remorse
- For trust to be rebuilt, the partner who committed the infidelity must take full responsibility for their actions and demonstrate genuine regret.
- **Ownership of Actions:** The person who betrayed their partner must take full ownership of their actions, without blaming external factors or circumstances. Acknowledging the wrongdoing and its consequences is essential for rebuilding trust.
- **Genuine Remorse:** Demonstrating genuine remorse involves more than just saying sorry. It means showing empathy for the pain caused, making amends, and being committed to changing behavior. Genuine remorse also involves a willingness to work on the underlying issues that led to the infidelity.
- Establishing Transparency and Openness
- Restoring trust requires a new level of transparency and openness in the relationship. This means creating an environment where both partners feel secure and informed.

Open Communication: Commit to regular, honest communication about feelings, concerns, and the state of the relationship. This includes discussing how each partner is coping with the aftermath of the infidelity and addressing any ongoing issues or insecurities.

- Sharing Information: The partner who committed the infidelity should be willing to share information about their actions and whereabouts, within reason. This transparency helps rebuild trust and reduces feelings of suspicion or doubt.

- Creating a Trust-Building Plan: Work together to create a trust-building plan that outlines specific actions and behaviors that will help restore confidence in the relationship. This might include regular check-ins, setting boundaries, or engaging in joint activities that strengthen the bond.

- Seeking Professional Assistance

- Professional support can be invaluable in the process of rebuilding trust. Therapy can provide both partners with the tools and guidance needed to address underlying issues and work through the healing process.

- Couples counseling provides a safe space for both partners to explore their feelings, improve communication, and develop strategies for rebuilding trust. A skilled therapist can help facilitate difficult conversations and provide support throughout the healing process.

- Personal therapy can be helpful for both partners as well. The person who committed the betrayal can work on understanding their motivations and addressing personal issues, while the betrayed partner can focus on processing their emotions and rebuilding self-esteem.

- Setting and Respecting Boundaries

- Boundaries play a crucial role in rebuilding trust by creating a framework for respectful and supportive behavior. Establishing clear boundaries helps both partners feel secure and respected.

- Discussing Boundaries: Both partners should discuss and agree on boundaries that will help rebuild trust. This might include guidelines for communication, interactions with others, or behaviors that need to change.

- Respecting Boundaries: It's essential for both partners to respect and adhere to the established boundaries. Consistently honoring these limits demonstrates commitment to the healing process and reinforces the trust-building effort.
- Rebuilding the Emotional Connection
- Rebuilding trust also involves rekindling the emotional connection that may have been damaged by the infidelity. Strengthening this connection helps reinforce the bond between partners and fosters a sense of intimacy and security.
- Quality Time Together: Spend quality time together engaging in activities that both partners enjoy. Shared experiences and positive interactions help rebuild the emotional connection and create new, positive memories.
- Expressing affection: On a regular basis, show your affection and appreciation for each other. Small gestures of love and gratitude can help reinforce the bond and remind both partners of the positive aspects of the relationship.

- Fostering Vulnerability: Create a safe space for both partners to be vulnerable and open with each other. Sharing fears, hopes, and dreams helps deepen the emotional connection and build trust.

Patience and Persistence

Rebuilding trust takes time and persistence. It's important to approach the process with patience and a commitment to long-term effort.

- Allowing Time for Healing: Understand that healing is a gradual process. Trust cannot be rebuilt overnight, and both partners need to allow themselves time to work through the pain and rebuild the relationship.

- Maintaining Effort: Throughout the healing process, both partners must be committed to sustaining their efforts. Consistent, positive actions and behaviors are key to restoring trust and rebuilding the relationship.

- Celebrating Progress: acknowledge and celebrate small victories and progress along the way. Recognizing the positive steps taken can provide motivation and reinforce the commitment to rebuilding trust.

Chapter 6

Leaving a Cheater

When I discovered my partner's betrayal, the emotional upheaval was overwhelming. I knew that staying in the relationship would only prolong the pain and hinder my path to healing. Deciding to end it was one of the hardest choices I've ever made, but it was necessary for my well-being. This chapter outlines my journey through the process of leaving and rebuilding my life.

The first step was to clarify my decision. I spent weeks reflecting on my feelings and the reasons behind my choice. I had to be certain that ending the relationship was the right decision for me. This self-reflection involved journaling my thoughts and talking to close friends who had been supportive throughout the ordeal.

Once I was clear about my decision, I planned how to communicate it. I decided that a face-to-face conversation was the most respectful approach. I prepared what I wanted to say, focusing on being honest and direct about my reasons for ending the relationship. It was essential for me to express my decision clearly to avoid any misunderstandings or false hope.

I reached out to a therapist for guidance and emotional support. They helped me navigate the complexities of the breakup and provided strategies for managing the emotional fallout. Having a support system was invaluable during this challenging time.

On the day of the breakup conversation, I chose a quiet, private setting where we could talk without interruptions. It was important to me that we both had the space to express ourselves calmly. I was honest and direct, stating clearly that I was ending the relationship and explaining the reasons behind my decision. I avoided sugar-coating or giving false hope, which I believed was crucial for both of us to move on.

Setting boundaries was another key aspect of the conversation. I communicated that, for the time being, I needed to limit or cut off contact to give both of us the space to heal. This decision was not made out of anger but as a necessary step for personal recovery.

Ending a relationship involves more than just emotional considerations; there are practical aspects to address. My partner and I had shared living arrangements and finances, so I needed to manage these logistical issues.

I began by separating our finances. This involved closing joint accounts, settling any shared debts, and arranging for the fair division of assets. It was a meticulous process, but essential for establishing financial independence.

Finding a new living arrangement was another significant step. I began searching for a new apartment and made arrangements for moving out. Coordinating the move was stressful, but having a plan helped me manage the transition smoothly.I also updated legal documents that included my partner's name, such as my will and insurance policy, to reflect my new situation.

The emotional aftermath of ending the relationship was intense. I allowed myself to grieve the loss, experiencing a range of emotions from sadness to relief. I recognized the importance of giving myself permission to feel and process these emotions at my own pace.

During this time, I leaned heavily on my support system. Friends and family provided comfort and encouragement, and my therapist offered invaluable guidance as I navigated my feelings and began to heal.

I also prioritized self-care. I reconnected with hobbies that had been sidelined and focused on my health. Simple activities like going for walks and practicing mindfulness helped manage stress and emotional pain.

Creating a new routine was essential for moving forward. I redesigned my living space to create a sense of renewal and signal the beginning of a new chapter in my life. This small act of change helped me feel a sense of fresh start.

I refocused on personal goals and interests that I had put on hold during the relationship. Reconnecting with my career aspirations and personal hobbies brought me fulfillment and a renewed sense of purpose.

Setting new boundaries in my interactions and relationships was crucial. I established clear limits to protect my well-being and foster healthy connections moving forward.

As I began to heal, I took time to reflect on the lessons learned from the relationship and the breakup. This reflection helped me gain insights into what I wanted and needed in future relationships.

I stayed open to new opportunities and experiences, embracing the possibility of growth and positive change. Building a positive support network of friends and family who uplifted and encouraged me played a significant role in this process.

Leaving a cheater was undoubtedly challenging, but it was also a catalyst for personal growth and a healthier future. My journey through the breakup and the steps I took to move forward helped me reclaim my life and embrace new beginnings

Deciding to end a relationship with someone who has been unfaithful is a difficult and often painful choice. It involves not only dealing with the immediate emotional fallout but also navigating the practical aspects of ending the relationship and moving forward. In this chapter, we'll explore practical guidance for ending a relationship with a cheater, ensuring that you do so in a way that prioritizes your well-being and sets you up for a healthier future.

Preparing for the Breakup

Preparation is key to managing the breakup process effectively. It involves both emotional and practical steps to ensure that you are ready to handle the complexities of ending the relationship.

- **Clarify Your Decision**: Make sure that ending the relationship is the right decision for you. Reflect on your feelings and the reasons behind your choice to ensure that it is made with clarity and confidence.

- **Plan Your Approach:** Decide how you want to communicate your decision to your partner. Consider whether you want to have a face-to-face conversation, write a letter, or use another method that feels appropriate for the situation. Prepare what you want to say, focusing on being clear and direct.

- **Seek Support**: Reach out to friends, family, or a therapist for support as you prepare for the breakup. Having a support system can provide emotional stability and practical advice during this challenging time.

Having the Breakup Conversation

The actual conversation about ending the relationship should be handled with care and respect. It's important to communicate your decision clearly while maintaining your dignity and composure.

- Choose the Right Time and Place: Pick a time and place where you can have an uninterrupted, private conversation. Avoid breaking up in a public place or during a heated moment to ensure that both parties can express themselves calmly.

- Be Honest and Direct: Clearly communicate your decision to end the relationship and the reasons behind it. Avoid vague explanations or giving false hope. Being honest helps both partners understand the situation and begin the process of moving on.

- Set Boundaries: After communicating your decision, establish clear boundaries for the future. This might include limiting or cutting off contact to allow both partners to heal and move forward.

Handling the Practical Aspects

Ending a relationship involves more than just the emotional conversation. There are practical aspects to consider, especially if you've shared living arrangements, finances, or other responsibilities.

- Separate Finances: If you share financial accounts or responsibilities, work to separate them. This might involve closing joint accounts, settling any shared debts, or arranging for the division of assets.

- Find a New Living Arrangement: If you live together, plan for a new living arrangement. This could involve finding a new place to live or making arrangements for one partner to move out. Make sure to coordinate the move in a way that minimizes stress and disruption.

- Update Legal Documents: If you have legal documents that include your partner's name, such as a will or insurance policy, update them to reflect your new situation.

Coping with the Emotional Aftermath

The emotional aftermath of ending a relationship with a cheater can be intense. It's important to give yourself the time and space to process your feelings and begin the healing process.

- Allow Yourself to Grieve: Ending a relationship involves a loss, and it's important to allow yourself to grieve. This might include feeling sadness, anger, or relief. Give yourself permission to experience these emotions and process them at your own pace.

- Seek Support: During this time, rely on your support system. Friends, family, or a therapist can provide emotional support and guidance as you navigate the aftermath of the breakup.

- Practice self-care: prioritize self-trouble to help manage stress and emotional pain. Do things you enjoy and focus on your health.

Establishing a New Routine

After ending the relationship, it's important to establish a new routine that supports your healing and personal growth.

- Create a Fresh Start: Redesign your living space or establish new routines to create a sense of renewal. This can help you move forward and signal a new chapter in your life.

- Pursue Personal Goals: Focus on personal goals and interests that may have been put on hold during the relationship. Reconnect with hobbies, career aspirations, or other aspects of your life that bring you fulfillment.

- Set New Boundaries: Establish new boundaries in your relationships and interactions to ensure that you are protecting your well-being and fostering healthy connections.

Moving Forward

Moving forward after ending a relationship with a cheater involves focusing on your personal growth and future happiness.

- Reflect on the Lessons Learned: Take time to reflect on the lessons learned from the relationship and the breakup. This can help you gain insights into what you want and need in future relationships.

- Stay Open to New Opportunities: As you heal, stay open to new opportunities and experiences. Embrace the possibility of growth and positive change as you move forward.

- Build a Positive Support Network: Surround yourself with supportive, positive people who uplift and encourage you. Building a strong support network can help you navigate the transition and foster a sense of community.

Chapter 7

Coping with the Emotional Impact of Infidelity

(Cheated Partner's Perspective)

When I discovered the infidelity, it felt like my world had shattered into a million pieces. The betrayal hit me hard, leaving me grappling with a complex mix of emotions: anger, sadness, confusion, and a deep sense of self-doubt. This chapter is a reflection on how I navigated these tumultuous feelings and found a path to emotional recovery.

The betrayal left me questioning my worth and attractiveness. I felt that if I had been more this or less that, maybe things would have been different. But I knew that I had to overcome these feelings to rebuild my self-esteem.

I started by reminding myself that the infidelity was not a reflection of my value or who I was. I took time to recognize my strengths, achievements, and the positive qualities that defined me. Writing down my accomplishments and positive attributes in a journal helped me see my worth clearly.

To challenge my negative thoughts, I practiced cognitive restructuring. When a thought like "I'm not good enough" surfaced, I questioned its validity and replaced it with affirmations of my worth. This process was gradual but helped me shift my mindset from self-criticism to self-affirmation.

I also embraced self-compassion. I treated myself with kindness, acknowledging that I was suffering and deserving of care. I engaged in self-care activities that made me feel good, like exercising, pursuing hobbies, and spending time with supportive friends. These activities reinforced a positive self-image and helped me reclaim my sense of self.

Managing the emotional aftermath of infidelity was a challenging journey. I had to allow myself to fully experience and process my emotions without judgment.

I gave myself permission to feel the pain, sadness, and anger. Suppressing these emotions would have only delayed my healing, so I let them flow naturally. Talking to a close friend and writing in my journal became essential outlets for expressing my feelings.

Seeking professional support was another crucial step. I began therapy to navigate my emotions and develop coping strategies. My therapist provided a safe space to explore my feelings, and their guidance helped me build resilience.

I developed a toolbox of coping strategies, including mindfulness and relaxation techniques. Practices like deep breathing and meditation became part of my routine, helping me manage stress and emotional pain. I set realistic expectations for myself, understanding that healing was a gradual process with its ups and downs.

Rebuilding trust in myself was a significant part of moving forward. I needed to regain confidence in my judgment and decisions. I reflected on the lessons learned from the betrayal and how they shaped my understanding of trust and relationships. This reflection helped me make more informed decisions moving forward.

Reconnecting with my intuition became important. I started paying more attention to my gut feelings and inner guidance, which helped me navigate new relationships and choices with greater clarity.

I also established clear boundaries to protect my emotional well-being. Knowing what I needed to feel safe and respected in future relationships was a crucial part of trusting myself again.

As I worked through the emotional impact of infidelity, I focused on embracing new opportunities for growth and fulfillment.

I leveraged this experience as a springboard for personal growth. I explored new interests and set personal goals that had been on the back burner. Investing in my own development brought a renewed sense of purpose and direction.

When I felt ready, I opened myself to the possibility of new relationships. I approached these connections with a healthier perspective, understanding that I deserved love and respect.

Building a supportive network of friends, family, and mentors was vital. Surrounding myself with positive, uplifting people provided emotional stability and encouragement as I moved forward.

- I celebrated every step of my progress, no matter how small. Recognizing and acknowledging my achievements boosted my confidence and reinforced my resilience.

- Ultimately, my goal was to find joy and fulfillment independent of the past hurt. I sought out activities and experiences that brought me happiness, such as traveling and spending time with loved ones.

- Practicing gratitude became a daily ritual. I kept a gratitude journal where I reflected on the positive aspects of my life. This practice helped shift my focus from past pain to present joy.

- I also created a vision for my future that aligned with my values and aspirations. Setting and pursuing meaningful goals provided a sense of purpose and direction, helping me look forward with optimism.

- Coping with the emotional impact of infidelity was undoubtedly a challenging journey, but it led me to a place of greater self-awareness and personal growth. Embracing new opportunities and finding joy in my life allowed me to move beyond the pain and create a fulfilling future.

- Experiencing infidelity can leave deep emotional scars. As the partner who was cheated on, you may face a complex array of feelings, including anger, sadness, guilt, and confusion. Coping with these emotions is a crucial part of healing and moving forward. This chapter will explore how to manage these emotions, overcome self-doubt and insecurity, and ultimately find a path to emotional recovery.

Overcoming self-doubt and insecurity

- Infidelity often leads to self-doubt and insecurity, as the betrayal can make you question your worth and attractiveness. Addressing these feelings is essential for rebuilding your self-esteem and confidence.

- Recognize Your Worth: Understand that the infidelity is not a reflection of your value or worth as a person. Your partner's actions are a result of their choices and issues, not a reflection of who you are. Remind yourself of your strengths, abilities, and successes.

- Challenge Negative Thoughts: Identify when you have negative thoughts about yourself and challenge them. Ask yourself if these thoughts are based on facts or emotions. Cognitive distortions, such as all-or-nothing thinking or personalizing betrayal, can exacerbate self-doubt. Reframe these thoughts to focus on your positive attributes and achievements.

- Embrace self-compassion: Treat yourself with kindness throughout this trying period. Offer yourself the same compassion and understanding that you would extend to a friend in a similar situation. Self-compassion involves recognizing your suffering, understanding that you are not alone, and offering yourself kindness.

- Engage in Self-Care: Prioritize activities that boost your self-esteem and make you feel positive about yourself. This might include pursuing hobbies, exercising, or spending time with supportive friends and family. Engaging in self-care can help reinforce a positive self-image.

Managing emotions and healing

Managing the emotional impact of infidelity involves acknowledging and processing your feelings in a healthy way. It's important to give yourself permission to feel and work through your emotions constructively.

- Allow Yourself to Feel: It's normal to experience a wide range of emotions, including anger, sadness, and betrayal. Allow these emotions to pass without criticizing yourself. Suppressing or ignoring your feelings can delay the healing process.

- Express Your Emotions: Discover healthy ways to express your feelings. This might include talking to a trusted friend, writing in a journal, or engaging in creative outlets like art or music. You may analyze and let go of your sentiments by expressing them.

- Seek Professional Support: Consider seeking therapy or counseling to help you navigate the emotional impact of infidelity. A therapist can provide a safe space to explore your feelings, develop coping strategies, and work through the trauma of the betrayal.

- Identify and put into practice coping mechanisms that are effective for you in order to develop coping skills. This might include mindfulness practices, relaxation techniques, or engaging in activities that bring you joy and relaxation. Developing a toolbox of coping strategies can help you manage stress and emotional pain.

- Set realistic expectations. Recognize that getting over an affair takes time. It's normal to have positive days and adverse days as you work through your emotions. Set realistic expectations for yourself and be patient with your healing journey.

Rebuilding trust in yourself

- After experiencing infidelity, rebuilding trust in yourself is crucial for moving forward. This means trusting your own judgment and decisions as you navigate your healing and future relationships.

- Your Experiences: Consider what you learned and how it influenced your perception of trust and relationships. Apply these insights to guide your decisions and actions as you move forward.

- When making decisions, reconnect with your intuition and trust your instincts. Your gut feelings and inner guidance can be valuable in helping you navigate future relationships and choices.

- Set Boundaries: Establish and maintain boundaries that protect your emotional well-being. Knowing your limits and standing firm on what you need to do to feel safe and respected in future relationships are part of trusting yourself.

Moving Forward and Embracing New Opportunities

- As you work through the emotional impact of infidelity, it's important to look forward and embrace new opportunities for growth and fulfillment.

- Focus on Personal Development: Make the most of this experience by going inside and learning about yourself. Explore new interests, set personal goals, and invest in your own development and well-being.

- Open Yourself to New Relationships: When you feel ready, open yourself to the possibility of new relationships. Approach new connections with a healthy perspective, recognizing that you are deserving of love and respect.

- Create and maintain a supportive network of friends, family, and mentors who uplift and encourage you. A strong support network can provide emotional stability and positive reinforcement as you move forward.

- **Celebrate Your Progress:** Acknowledge and celebrate the progress you make on your healing journey. Recognizing and celebrating your achievements, no matter how small, can boost your confidence and reinforce your sense of resilience.

- **Finding joy and fulfillment**: Ultimately, the goal is to find joy and fulfillment in your life, independent of the past hurt. Embracing life's positive aspects and creating new, meaningful experiences can help you move beyond the pain of infidelity.

- Engage in Joyful Activities: Pursue activities and experiences that bring you joy and satisfaction. This might include hobbies, travel, or spending time with loved ones. Engaging in positive experiences can help shift your focus from past pain to present happiness.

- Practice thankfulness and keep your attention on the good things in your life. Keeping a gratitude journal or regularly reflecting on what you are thankful for can help shift your mindset and enhance your overall sense of well-being.

- Create a Vision for Your Future: Envision and work towards a fulfilling future that aligns with your values and aspirations. Setting and pursuing goals that are meaningful to you can provide a sense of purpose and direction.

Chapter 8

Navigating a Complex Healing Landscape

After the storm of betrayal had settled, I was left to navigate the complex and often overwhelming landscape of healing. The emotional aftermath of infidelity left me grappling with deep pain, self-doubt, and a yearning for clarity. This chapter reflects on how I embraced my healing journey, rebuilt trust and self-esteem, and moved forward with renewed confidence and joy.

The first step in my healing process was to accept that it would be a journey, not a quick fix. I needed to allow myself the time and space to heal at my own pace, without rushing or forcing the process.

I gave myself permission to feel all the emotions that came with the betrayal—anger, sadness, confusion, and even moments of hope. I knew that healing wasn't linear, and I embraced the idea that it was okay to have both good days and challenging ones.

Support became a cornerstone of my healing journey. I reached out to a therapist who helped me navigate my emotions and provided valuable insights. Joining a support group offered me a sense of connection and understanding from others who had faced similar challenges. These support systems validated my feelings and guided me through the ups and downs of my journey.

Patience was crucial. I learned to celebrate small victories and recognize progress, no matter how minor. Each step forward, no matter how small, was a testament to my resilience and commitment to healing.

Restoring trust, both in myself and in others, was a significant part of my healing process. I had to address how the betrayal had shaken my confidence and reframe my approach to relationships.

Rebuilding trust in the context of the relationship was a complex task. If I had chosen to continue, it would have involved honest communication, transparency, and a commitment to change. However, for me, moving on meant focusing on rebuilding trust in future relationships, grounded in self-awareness and healthy boundaries.

Restoring my self-esteem was a vital aspect of this phase. I worked diligently to recognize my worth beyond the betrayal. I engaged in self-care activities that affirmed my value, such as pursuing hobbies I loved and surrounding myself with supportive friends who reminded me of my strengths.

Setting healthy boundaries was a key part of my recovery. I established clear limits in my interactions and relationships to ensure my emotional well-being was protected. These boundaries helped me maintain respect for myself and foster healthier connections with others.

As I began to heal, I focused on moving forward with a sense of hope and determination. I was ready to embrace new possibilities and explore what the future held.

I made myself available to new possibilities and experiences. I started exploring interests I had neglected and set personal goals that reignited my passion for life. This exploration was not just about distraction but about genuine growth and fulfillment.

Personal development became a central theme in my journey. I reflected on the lessons I had learned from the betrayal and applied them to my life. This reflection fostered resilience and self-discovery, helping me grow stronger and more self-aware.

Creating a vision for my future was a transformative step. I developed a clear sense of what I wanted to achieve and the kind of life I aspired to live. Setting and working towards these goals provided me with purpose and direction, allowing me to move forward with confidence.

Finding joy and celebrating my progress were essential components of my healing journey. I learned to embrace the positive aspects of my life and acknowledge the strides I had made.

I made a habit of celebrating achievements, no matter how small. Each milestone, whether it was finding a new hobby or reconnecting with friends, was a cause for celebration. This practice reinforced my sense of accomplishment and motivated me to continue moving forward.

Making time for the things I enjoyed became a top priority. I pursued passions that filled me with happiness and fulfillment, such as traveling and spending quality time with loved ones. These joyful experiences helped shift my focus from past pain to present contentment.

Practicing gratitude also played a significant role. I kept a gratitude journal where I reflected on the positive aspects of my life. This practice helped me shift my perspective and enhanced my overall sense of well-being.

Navigating the aftermath of infidelity was undoubtedly challenging, but it led me to a place of profound personal growth and resilience. Embracing the healing journey, rebuilding trust and self-esteem, and finding joy in the present allowed me to move beyond the pain and create a fulfilling, hopeful future.

Navigating the aftermath of infidelity and the journey toward healing is a profound and transformative process. It requires not only addressing the immediate pain and emotional fallout but also embarking on a path of self-discovery, growth, and renewal.

This conclusion aims to encapsulate the key takeaways from our exploration of Post-Infidelity Stress Disorder (PISD) and provide a roadmap for moving forward with clarity and resilience.

1.   Embracing the Healing Journey

Healing from infidelity is a journey that involves confronting and processing a range of emotions, from anger and sadness to confusion and hope. Embracing this journey means acknowledging that healing takes time and effort, and that it's okay to move at your own pace.

- Allow Yourself to Heal: Recognize that healing is a gradual process. It's important to give yourself permission to experience and work through your emotions without rushing the process. Trust that with time, support, and self-care, you will find your way forward.

- Seek Support: Utilize the support systems available to you, whether it's through therapy, support groups, or trusted friends and family. Support from others can provide validation, guidance, and a sense of connection as you navigate your healing journey.

- Practice patience. Recognize that the healing process after infidelity is not a straightforward journey. It's crucial to have patience with oneself since there will be ups and downs. Appreciate incremental gains and advancements made along the path.

Building trust and self-esteem

Restoring trust, both in others and in yourself, is a crucial aspect of healing from infidelity. It involves rebuilding confidence, setting healthy boundaries, and fostering positive relationships.

- Rebuild Trust: If you choose to continue the relationship, focus on rebuilding trust through honest communication, transparency, and commitment to change. For those moving on, rebuilding trust in future relationships requires a foundation of self-awareness and healthy boundaries.

- Restore self-esteem: Work on rebuilding your self-esteem by recognizing your worth and challenging negative self-perceptions. Engage in self-care practices and pursue activities that affirm your value and capabilities.

- Create healthy boundaries: Define and uphold limits that safeguard your emotional health. Clear boundaries are essential for maintaining healthy relationships and ensuring that your needs and values are respected.

Moving Forward with Confidence

Moving forward after experiencing infidelity involves embracing new opportunities, pursuing personal growth, and creating a fulfilling future. It's about looking ahead with a sense of hope and determination.

- Embrace new possibilities: Open yourself to new experiences and opportunities. Whether it's exploring new interests, pursuing personal goals, or forming new relationships, staying open to the future can lead to growth and fulfillment.
- Foster Personal Growth: Use the experience as an opportunity for personal development. Reflect on the lessons learned and apply them to your life, fostering growth, resilience, and self-discovery.
- Create a Vision for Your Future: Develop a vision for your future that aligns with your values and aspirations. As you progress, setting and achieving goals may give you a feeling of direction and purpose.

4.   Celebrating Progress and Finding Joy

Finding joy and celebrating progress are essential components of healing and moving forward. Embrace the positive aspects of your life and acknowledge the strides you've made on your journey.

- Celebrate Achievements: Recognize and celebrate your accomplishments, no matter how small. Celebrating progress reinforces your sense of accomplishment and motivates you to continue moving forward.
- Foster Joy: Participate in activities that bring you happiness and a sense of fulfillment. Pursuing passions, spending time with loved ones, and finding joy in everyday moments can enhance your overall well-being.
- Practice Gratitude: To cultivate a practice of gratitude, focus on the positive aspects of your life. Reflecting on what you're thankful for can shift your perspective and enhance your sense of contentment.

Conclusion

Recovering from infidelity is a multifaceted and profoundly personal journey. It requires courage, resilience, and a commitment to self-care and personal growth. While the path may be challenging, it also holds the potential for profound transformation and renewal.

As you navigate the terrain of healing, remember that you have the strength and resources to overcome the pain and build a fulfilling future. Trust in yourself, seek support, and embrace the opportunities for growth and happiness that lie ahead. You are entitled to love, respect, and a life abundant in joy and fulfillment.

Thank you for joining me on this journey through understanding and healing from post-infidelity stress disorder (PISD). May you find strength, resilience, and hope as you move forward and embrace a brighter future.